AMERICAN ARWROLOGY

The Science of
ALL-OUT
HAND-TO-HAND
FIGHTING

Fred C. Bauer

American Arwrology

Copyright Fred C. Bauer (2011)
First edition. Published July 2011
First softcover edition. Published January 2013

ISBN: 978-0-9549494-3-3

CQB PUBLICATIONS (UK) LIMITED
PO Box 8256, Harlow, Essex CM19 4WY England.
Website: www.cqbpublications.com

Cover design by Mark Savill. Cover concept Mark Savill, Paul R. Child & Fred C. Bauer.

The "Sword, Pen and Wheel" design is the trademark of CQB Publications (UK) Limited and may not be used without permission. Designed for CQB Publications by Mark Savill.

Disclaimer

Both the author and the publishers of this book wish to emphasise that this book and all its contents are intended for academic and general information purposes only.

Readers should not make use of any of the information in this book without the supervision of a qualified instructor.

It is always advisable before practicing any martial art or combative system to seek advice from your medical doctor.

The author and the publisher of this book accept no liability for any loss, damage or injury sustained.

The publisher wishes to point out that the carrying of an edged weapon in public places in the United Kingdom is a criminal offence, which can be punishable with a prison sentence. The publisher supports the prosecution and maximum penalties under law for any edged weapon related crime, in any legal jurisdiction.

The publishers do not endorse or suggest the use of "live" edged weapons in training involving members of the public. Safe training alternatives are available and should be used appropriately.

CONTENTS

Dedication to their memory and their combative genius.

Dr. Gordon E. Perrigard,1st Regent
(1915 - 2000)
Canadian Society of Arwrology

Robert C. Kasper, (1950 - 2006)
1st Regent American Society of
Arwrology and Founder
Gung Ho Chuan Association

AMERICAN ARWROLOGY

FOREWORD

It was the fall of 1995 when I was first introduced to the Gung Ho Chuan Association (GHCA). At that time I had a little over six years experience at a local Police Department in New Jersey. A few years into my Law Enforcement career I realized that some of my training wasn't as realistic as needed. I was looking for a fighting system that was practical and truly effective for the streets. I found the solution to my concerns with Bob Kasper and the GHCA.

During 1995, my Patrol Supervisor, Sergeant-First-Class Fred Killian, began to train with the GHCA. After a few months of training he introduced me to some of the techniques and principles of the Association. Prior to each shift, we would review these methods to prepare ourselves for patrol.

My interest was piqued and in February of 1996 I was invited to train with Bob Kasper and his Association. After becoming a member of the GHCA I was privileged to share the close-combat system with interested members of my Department and its Tactical Unit. Thereafter, I was afforded the opportunity to travel with Bob and assist him with instructing law enforcement agencies, the United States Marine Corps, the United Nations International Police Task Force and members of the Federal Air Marshals. Internationally I also represented the GHCA in Bosnia and Kenya while working on protective details.

In 2001 Bob was granted permission by the Canadian Society of Arwrologists (CSA) to found the American Society of Arwrologists. Afterwards, he selected seven loyal instructors he had personally trained and together they tested the principles and techniques developed by Dr. Perrigard. I was honored to be among the chosen seven and to receive an original, signed copy of Dr. Perrigard's Arwrology directly from Bob.

FOREWORD

In January 2004 after years of studying Arwrology, the CSA endorsed Bob's request to add Arwrology to the already proven GHCA curriculum. Bob and the chosen instructors then introduced Arwrology to the rest of the Association membership. At this time, Bob publicly announced that I would be his successor.

Several months later, Bob moved from New Jersey to Pennsylvania, leaving me and co-founder John Watson to maintain the GHCA. However, Bob continued to research the concepts of Arwrology and would communicate his findings to us. We would then put the new concepts to task through practical appliance at the GHCA Training Center in New Jersey. Our results would be transmitted back to Bob who would decide whether to introduce it to the membership, discard it, or revamp it for further study.

From then until 2006, Bob and I, as his chosen successor, would travel and train together, constantly communicating with one another to discuss the fighting techniques of the American Society of Arwrologists/GHCA, all for the advancement of the organization. However, in early July 2006 Bob was diagnosed with brain and lung cancer. Although he had been the quintessential warrior in the past, having beaten cancer on three prior occasions, this new diagnosis was terminal.

In Mid-September of that year, family and friends from all over the country and Canada gathered with Bob to celebrate his life and say their goodbyes. Michael Thomson, 2nd Regent of the Canadian Society of Arwroloigists, declared that the CSA was dissolving and was turning the direction of Arwrology over to Robert Kasper. After this statement, Bob stood and announced to all present that he was stepping down due to his health and turning everything over to his successor, Fred Bauer.

Later, during this gathering, he gave me several binders filled with his personal research, notes, writings and an outline for a book....
....American Arwrology.

AMERICAN ARWROLOGY

The next day I read the contents of the binders and realized how much time and effort Bob had put into his research. It was then that I made a commitment to myself to complete the research and complete American Arwrology. A couple weeks later, I met with Bob at his home in Pennsylvania and he presented me with his personal copy of Dr. Perrigard's Arwrology. The book was filled with his notes and research for American Arwrology and he asked that I finish what he had started.

At the end of our visit, I assisted Bob up the stairs from his office to his living room. We shared a parting glance and a hug goodbye. It would be the last time I would see my friend, mentor and the 1st Regent of the American Society of Arwrologisits, alive.

Robert C. Kasper died October 6th 2006.

Since Bob's death I have continued to review, study and train from the notes, writings and research I was given by him. From all this I am proud to have fulfilled the wish of two men, Dr. Gordon Perrigard and Robert C. Kasper; the wish that the art and science of Arwrology be promulgated as an All-Out Hand-to-Hand Fighting System.

ACKNOWLEDGEMENTS

The Preface, Introduction, Chapter 1 and most of Chapter 2 are Robert Kasper's own words and are based upon his personal experiences. I completed the remainder of this book based upon the notes and outline Bob provided me along with additional research, studies and practice I have personally conducted since October 6th 2006. My work continues to be guided by two promises: the promise I made to Bob to honor his request that I complete this book and the promise I made to myself to complete it in the manner that would honor the legacies of Dr. Perrigard, Robert C. Kasper and all the members of the Gung Ho Chuan Association and the American Society of Arwrologists who continue to contribute to the art and science of Arwrology.

I would like to recognize and personally thank and remember all the members of the Canadian Society of Arwrologists; you will never be forgotten. To the members of the American Society of Arwrologists and the Gung Ho Chuan Association who assisted me in completing this work, I am grateful for your unconditional assistance. To the members of the GHCA who were members before me, especially the co-founders, Joe Kanabrocki and John Watson, and all the current members, your continued loyalty and support are greatly appreciated. To Douglas Rodriguez, photographer for this volume. Finally, to my truly understanding wife, Heather, whose patience, sacrifices and unfailing support permits me to continue to take this endeavor into the future, a heartfelt thank you.

Fred C. Bauer

2nd Regent, American Society of Arwrologists

The Canadian Society of Arwrologists

16th. September 2006

AB SUM

Dear Bob,

As I grew older, my greatest concern was the spectre of the possible dissolution of the C. S. A. and with it, the demise of the art and science of Arwrology.

This proud and effective society was in danger of being under-mined by the ageing of it's members and the lack of suitable young replacements.

Determined not to sacrifice my principles, I expanded the search for my successor to the whole North American Continent.

I finally compiled a list of four prospective candidates and asked some of our senior members to investigate each candidate's credentials.

When the checks were completed we met and compared our evaluations.

Those candidates whose resumes were either extravagant or inaccurate, indeed in one case were extravagantly inaccurate, did not receive further consideration.

The sole survivor was not only recognized as competent in several areas of martial arts and disciplines but also had a solid grounding in personnel selection and administration.

As my health was rapidly failing I named Mike Thomson Second Regent of the C. S. A. and charged him with assisting the unanimously selected candidate, Bob Kasper, with the founding of The American Society of Arwrologists and naming Bob Kasper, First Regent.

Mike was also charged with overseeing the transfer of my library and some artifacts to The A. S. A. and assisting them in their endeavours.

From the beyond, as always; I send my warmest wishes to you and to all the members of The A. S. A. and respectfully counsel you to always be too careful.

Do not be afraid "to do the right as you see the right". I will always be present.

The Doc.

Note: The author of this letter was Not Dr. Gordon Eric Perrigard.

This letter was composed using a collage of actual comments and statements made by "The Doc" to various members of The C. S. A. during the above time period.

Anon.

Postscript:

Bob, it's been almost five tough years since you became the First Regent of The A. S. A. During this period you have built a strong foundation for the A. S. A. and are well on the way to developing a formidable cadre of Arwrologists to assist you in the judicious propagation of this art and science.

Your Canadian Confreres are astonished by this amazing rate of progress. It confirms the trust and confidence that "The Doc" expressed when he selected you for this task. It's fair to say that Arwrology now has a better and stronger presence than ever before. We salute you for your efforts and expertize and hope this progress continues.

We send our warmest wishes and respectfully counsel you to always be too careful.

Sincerely,   The "Doc's" Post-Obit Seal

Mike Thomson

2nd. Regent C.S.A.

American Society of Arwrologists
Si Vis Pacem, Para Bellum
Inaugurated 2001

05 January 2004

To Whom It May Concern:

I, *Robert Charles Kasper*, <u>Founder and 1st Regent of the American Society of Arwrologists</u>, <u>Founder/1st Generation 'Head of Family' of the American Karate Jutsu Association</u>, being of sound mind and memory, declare this document to be my last request concerning the American Society of Arwrologists and the American Karate Jutsu Association.

In the case of my death I declare *Fred Carl Bauer, Jr.* (SSN   ), as my successor as <u>Regent of the American Society of Arwrologists</u> which was granted to me December 10, 2001 by the Canadian Society of Arwrolgists. I also declare *Fred Carl Bauer, Jr.* my successor as <u>'Head of Family' of the American Karate Jutsu Association</u> which was granted to me January 1, 1992 by the Independent Karate Schools of America.

Fred Carl Bauer, Jr. is to assume the same rank/time-in-grade that I possess at the time of my death. He is also to assume the title 2nd Regent American Society of Arwrologists and 2nd Generation 'Head of Family' of the American Karate Jutsu Association with all the rights, honors, responsibilities, and privileges associated with these titles.

I swear that on the above date, I signed and executed this instrument willingly and as a free and voluntary act, and at the time of sound mind and under no constraint or undue influence. This legal document supercedes all previous documents of the above mentioned subject.

Robert C. Kasper, M.A.S.A
Founder and First Regent
American Society of Arwrologists
Founder/1st Generation/7th DBB
'Head of Family'
American Karate Jutsu Association

Patricia A. Kasper, Witness

ix

AMERICAN ARWROLOGY

PREFACE

It was the Winter of 1994 when I received a phone call from the then Gung Ho Chuan Association Historian Lawrence Kubacki. Fellow WW-2 era jiu-jitsu researcher Dave Kentner had located Samurai Jiu-Jitsu Master and author Dr. Gordon E. Perrigard of Montreal, Canada. Dr. Perrigard's book Arwrology, All-Out Hand-to-Hand Fighting was on my list to research so this was exciting news for me to receive.

Written in 1943 for the fighting man to help support the war effort, Perrigard's Arwrology was his interpretation of military hand-to-hand fighting based on his extensive knowledge of Samurai Jiu-Jitsu and the human anatomy as it applied to medical science. After a few correspondences with Dr. Perrigard, he was kind enough to send me one of his personal copies of Arwrology. This started me on a decade long research project of the art and science of Perrigard's style of all-out hand-to-hand fighting.

In 2000, five years after my initial contact, Dr. Perrigard passed away at the age of 85. Shortly thereafter, I was contacted by his successor and Arwrology student of over 50 years, Michael Thomson, 2nd Regent, Canadian Society of Arwrologists. It was at this time that Mr. Thomson informed me that one of "The Doc's" last wishes was that Arwrology would be propagated internationally and that I was the one whom he chose to take on the task. One year later in 2001 a special caucus of the Canadian Society of Arwrologists inaugurated the American Society of Arwrologists naming me, Founder and 1st Regent. Shortly thereafter I incorporated Dr. Perrigard's principles and techniques into the Gung Ho Chuan Association's Close Combat Program of Instruction. Once completed, I continued my research into Arwrology which took me on a path I never expected to travel. This journey resulted in unlocking the secrets of *"the study of the art and science of personal combat to the death."*[1] Thus, this book - American Arwrology, The Science of All-Out Hand-to-Hand Fighting, is born.

INTRODUCTION

My hand-to-hand combat journey started in 1969 while at Marine Corps Recruit Depot, Parris Island, North Carolina. It was there I received my first taste of all-out fighting via what I would call remnants of the Pat Dermott O'Neil, of Devil's Brigade fame, system of close combat.

The two techniques that stood out most and which are embedded in my brain to this day are attacking from the front which consisted of biting off the enemy's nose, and attacking from the rear which was the naked strangle hold. Not much of a close combat program of instruction but enough to get the idea of using a combination of an aggressive attitude and whatever form of brutality it takes to defeat the enemy.

After my four year military enlistment I spent a decade of Japanese martial arts training and 28 years of years of WW-2 era close combat training and research, the last ten being dedicated to the study of the principles and techniques of Arwrology. What I discovered throughout this 36 year career of hand-to-hand fighting is that when under extreme stress of violence the body is going to react to what it knows best. And what it knows best is what it has been trained to do the most. Some call this "muscle memory", others "familiar task transfer". Dr. Gordon E. Perrigard, 1st Regent, Canadian Society of Arwrologists called it - *"Auto Condition Reflex."*

In the preface of his 1943 book Arwrology, Dr. Perrigard states; *"Exercise should be designed to quicken fighting reflexes so that correct fighting will become automatic."*[1]. The theme of continuous practice to develop conditioned reflexes is emphasized throughout Dr. Perrigard's book, and is the theme which formed the foundation of my research for, and development of American Arwrology.

AMERICAN ARWROLOGY

"WHY ARWROLOGY?"

During my 36 years of training and research I have accumulated over 100 original works in the subject of old school jiu-jitsu dating as far back as the early 1900's. Also included are early military training films and countless pages of military and government files from the National Archives and Records Administration on the subject of close-combat. Also during this time, I had the privilege of training with, personal interviews, phone conversations and many letters from several World War Two era close combat instructors. Through this training and research I developed a set of beliefs that formed the foundation of my training. What attracted me to Arwrology was the verification of my beliefs all wrapped up in one neat little package. At this point I think it is important to mention that it is impossible for any man to exactly duplicate the technique of another. We can study the principles and know them like the back of our hand, mirror the instructor to the best of our physical ability, but because of our individual physical makeup we will never be like those we wish to imitate. In our effectiveness as a fighter we might wind up worse, or become better, but we will never be the same. As an expert in the medical field Dr. Perrigard understood this and thus stated,

"The methods may not be suitable for your size, weight and development. Slight variations may be necessary..." and,

"Because of the differences in size, weight and strength, among students and opponents, slight variations may be used, governed by the individual need..."[2]

During the past five years I've been under the tutelage of Dr. Perrigard's successor, 2nd Regent Mike Thomson, Fellow of the Canadian Society of Arwrologists. From my countless conversations with Mike Thomson I have realized that although a student of Dr. Perrigard for 50 years, Mike did not execute methods exactly the same as The Doc. In one of our conversations I asked, "Do you use a lot of knee blows?" Mike quickly answered "Yes, I did

"WHY ARWROLOGY?"

because of my height." This is exactly what The Doc was referring to in his statement above. The reason I'm mentioning this is that I do not want to give anyone the idea that this book is only Arwrology, *"a la" Perrigard*. It is not. The principles are Arwrology, the targets are Arwrology, the natural weapons are Arwrology, but the body movement is Bob Kasper's interpretation of Dr. Perrigard's Arwrology based on research from the training and information provided in the form of copies of the Doc's notes, original copies of students' notes, and training and interpretation of those through the tutelage of Dr. Perrigard successor, Mike Thomson. Also, it should be mentioned that The Doc wrote Arwrology during the War for the fighting man and therefore a portion of the book was dedicated to the military training oriented calisthenics to develop conditioned reflexes. I have substituted these exercises in favor of body movement based on Chinese exercises which duplicates Arwrology fighting movements. These exercises not only help develop automatic conditioned reflexes but also have health benefits as well.

EPITOME

This book, as the original, is an attempt to start the student on the study of all-out hand-to-hand fighting. Its main purpose is to give an understanding of the philosophy and techniques of Dr. Perrigard's original as I interpret it. Please understand that as a practitioner of hand-to-hand fighting for over three decades I have my own ideas on training, movement and power development which are infused into Arwrology. Thus, out of respect for The Doc's original work, I call it by a different name - American Arwrology.

In this work I have included the Arwrology principle of auto condition reflex, train both sides, and the endless knot. Also included are conditioning drills, such as body whips, knee blows and wall drills.

The reader will learn the main ingredients of hand-to-hand fighting technique and the D-55 blow power drill, which is the nuts and bolts of American Arwrology. Next will come the multiple striking variations of which are all based on auto conditioned reflex training. In the pages following the student will learn brutal throws and the death dealing Arwr locks. You must *"always be too careful"* when practicing these because *"necks and hearts may be broken easily by premature enthusiasm or horse play."*[1].

The final portion of the book is dedicated to a very important aspect of hand-to-hand fighting-combat: use of the Dragon Knife. This last part will also contain a daily training plan to begin the journey into the science of Arwrology.

At the end of World War Two the Canadian government deemed Dr. Gordon E. Perrigard's Arwrology too violent to continue to be printed and made available to the general public. Therefore, all printing plates were destroyed along with original manuscripts. Because of the first and only printing being in small numbers Arwrology has become an extremely rare book. This publishing of American Arwrology is my attempt to give you some insight into hand-to-hand fighting genius of Dr. Gordon Perrigard which for many has never been made available. I hope I have accomplished my goal.

CHAPTER 1

PRINCIPLES

What Is Arwrology?

Arwrology (pronounced R-ology) is derived from *"the old Welsh word, Arwr meaning Hero, All-Out Hand-to-Hand Fighter."* Thus, Arwrology can be defined as the Science of All-Out Hand-to-Hand Fighting. Or to be more accurate, based on its program of instruction and defined on Arwrology's back cover, *"It is the study of the science and art of personal combat to the death."* What exactly did Dr. Perrigard mean by personal combat to the death?

At the time of writing Arwrology, Dr. Perrigard had been a student of Samurai Jiu-Jitsu for 23 years. His mastering of that art plus his medical knowledge and natural fighting talents form the basis for his thoughts on what close combat should consist of. His conclusion and goal was all-out, whatever-it-takes, fighting to the death. His means for achieving this goal was to kill via vital area blows and death locks designed to cut off the oxygen and blood supply to the brain. Dr. Perrigard pulled no punches in his work Arwrology which may have been the reason for his book being outlawed only a few years after it was published.

"Arwrology...if the enemy is ever encountered, it will make you a killer. That's not a gentle thought, but we are in warring times. Self-Preservation is a strong sentiment. Who knows when the alternative of kill or be killed will be forced upon any of us. We fight for life and the four freedoms of the world." 1.

AMERICAN ARWROLOGY

In his introduction, Dr. Perrigard describes Arwrology as an amoeba drawing its victims into its nucleus to be destroyed.

"Arwrology is a death trap of which the student becomes the master...In Arwrology; the most important holds are the death dealing "Arwr" locks. They form the nucleus of the science...Second in importance are the blows and kicks, many of which are fatal, they form an accretion around the "Arwr" locks...The rest of the science includes nerve grips, throws and locks...Feeding the deadly centre...They are designed to lead the opponent into position for receiving death blows or the death locks." 2

Later, in his chapter on blows, Dr. Perrigard states his goal for all-out hand-to-hand fighting; *"Always aim for an Arwr lock."*3

I want to teach the principles behind the art and science. Again, these are my interpretations based on my decade research. One can read Arwrology and get a very general idea of the master's creation, but only through extensive reading, research, and daily practice with practical experimentation will you begin to understand the true essence of Arwrology.

Auto Conditioned Reflexes

A repeated theme throughout Arwrology is the development of Automatic Conditioned Reflexes. What do we mean by Auto Conditioned Reflexes? In the case of combat it is an automatic neuro-muscular response to an act of violence that we have conditioned through consistent training. An everyday example of this would be the quick application of your automobile's brakes when someone suddenly stops in front of you. When we first learn to drive, we conscientiously applied the brakes to slow down and come to a complete stop. Over the years from constant repetition of this physical act we condition those

PRINCIPLES

reflexes to become automatic whenever the need arises. Think about what you do all day, every day and you'll give yourself hundreds of examples of Automatic Conditioned Reflexes.

How do we develop Automatic Conditioned Reflexes? Repetition, repetition, repetition. There is a new "old" adage that says less is more. What this means is that it is better to know less technique very well, than to know more technique not so well. I agree wholeheartedly with this adage as long as the more technique is substituted for more repetitions and preferably every day. Do not use the less is more adage as an excuse to train less. What is a better method to develop an automatic conditioned reflex-throwing 1000 forehand elbows every tenth day or throwing 100 blows every day for ten days? I believe the answer is obvious. Everyday moderate training will do more to develop conditioned reflexes than thousands or repetitions done once a week. Dr. Perrigard understood the need for repetition and was very vocal about it throughout Arwrology.

"Repeat these actions over and over."
"Repeat this procedure over and over..."
"Repeat the cycles of blows over and over..."
"Practice this until it becomes an automatic habit."
"The point is to practice and develop conditioned reflexes..."
"A fast reaction time is of paramount importance in Arwrology."4.

In the following chapters I will present drills to develop automatic conditioned reflexes while conditioning the body to maximize speed and power. By this time you may be asking how in the world can you develop automatic

3

conditioned reflexes for all the possible violent scenarios you may come across? The answer is not the individual techniques itself but in the general body that carries the technique. It's developing those neuro-muscular movements that are used to execute the majority of strikes, throws and chokes. This is the best summed up by The Doc himself and will also lead us into the next principle-Speed.

"You must shorten your reaction time in all fighting methods described. At first practice the methods slowly and exactly. Gradually speed up every movement. Develop little movements and reflexes into habits, so you may act without thinking. A good ARWR-MAN develops an automatic technique that takes care of most of his fighting methods."[5]

Speed

As with Automatic Conditioned Reflexes, Dr. Perrigard emphasized the importance of speed throughout Arwrology. In fact, he opens Part 1 with, *"Speed is very important...If anyone can see what you are doing, you are doing it too slowly!"* So, how do we develop speed in our reaction and delivery of techniques? Repetition, repetition, repetition.

As the group of muscles used in a certain movement become well developed through consistent practice, they are able to respond in a more efficient manner thus having the ability to move faster. Because that group of muscles has been trained to a conditioned reflex the response time from "pulling the trigger" to when the strike hits it target is greatly decreased. So we can see automatic conditioned reflexes and speed go hand in hand. When you develop one you develop the other.[6]

"....practice and develop conditioned reflexes to speed up your fighting movements."[7]

PRINCIPLES

Know Both Sides

Training to master techniques on both sides of the body has always been an important part of my hand-to-hand program of instruction. This is another principle Dr. Perrigard emphasized throughout Arwrology. *"Knowing Both Sides (K.B.S.) after learning a method using the right or the left side of your body, practice the same method again, using the other side."*[8]

I know there are close combat instructors out there who only teach "strong side" methods, but it is my opinion, and apparently Dr. Perrigard's, that this is doing a great disservice to their students. When fighting for your life, you should not have a weak side. What happens when your strong side is injured? What happens when you are attacked on your weak side, and need to momentarily physically engage from that side in order to draw a weapon? What happens when your strong side is subdued? *"Be an ambidextrous fighter. Have no weak side."*[9]

Besides the practical application it makes sense to know both sides, there are other reasons to strengthen the weak parts of your body. By strengthening the weak link, it strengthens the whole. When you train both sides your technique will become quicker, stronger, and evenly balanced. Also, and most importantly, you double the amount of fighting methods without doubling the amount of individual technique.

Dr. Perrigard knew the tremendous fighting value of knowing both sides and the advantage it gave an Arwr-man over an average fighter. He brings this principle to light throughout his writing and also his teaching. I, as did The Doc, will touch more on his subject throughout this book only because,

"I cannot repeat enough the importance of being able to do these methods from either side of your opponent."[10]

Endless Knot

The Arwrology principle of the endless knot is best defined as; *"Its methods can be linked up together so that if one happens to fail, another, generally more deadly, is ready to take its place immediately, until ultimately your opponent is snared in a death-lock."*11

This approach reflects the dynamic thinking of Arwrology. Deadly fighting methods (techniques) can be linked together and also substituted one for another when the need arises. *"...a student..is started on a series of hardening exercises which include methods of striking an opponent with everything from the edge of his hand to the heel of his feet..Then comes the endless interlocking sequences of...nerve grips...vindictive throws... death dealing Arwr locks."*12

At this point you may be skeptical, and that's a good thing. In fact, being skeptical is our next principle. You are probably thinking that in order to have a fighting system of interlocking strikes, grips, throws and chokes you would need an encyclopedia of technique and therefore, how can you train all those techniques to be automatic conditioned reflex? Very simple, and as you progress through American Arwrology you will begin to see how easily this can be achieved by daily training on both sides to develop those conditioned reflexes. If you concentrate on perfecting each individual technique you will never achieve the endless knot. If you concentrate on perfecting the body movement behind each individual technique, then you will understand the science of Arwrology and master the principle of the endless knot.

*"The beauty of Arwrology is that nearly all the methods can interlock with each other or reinforce each other. So that if one method happens to fail, another should be ready for just such emergency. Arwrology is a rhythmical science, with interlocking holds and follow-up methods. As your knowledge of the arts progresses, your actions become more rhythmical, deadly and automatic."*13

6

PRINCIPLES

The principle of the endless knot was so important to the Society of Arwrologists that it was placed on their 1940 logo and remains there to this day.

Be Skeptical

Dr. Perrigard was a realist. He understood the dynamics of fighting, the differences in individuals, the enemy's resistance and his will to survive, and the resilience of the human body. *"When fighting one of the enemy, you have to expect terrific resistance, as the man is fighting for his life.."*14 He did not want students of Arwrology to believe everything they saw or read, including his own work. Instead, the Doc wanted them to have self-confidence in their own skills, not his, and therefore he admonished them to be skeptical of everything.

*"Does it Work? Be Skeptical. Do not trust every hold you have read about or have seen. Try it yourself on different people. Put it to the test. If you find some of these methods do not work as well as expected, it may be that you have misunderstood some important point. Read the instructions again. The methods may not be suitable for your size, weight and development. Slight adjustments may be necessary."*15

What The Doc is saying is that if something does not work for you, you either misunderstood the technique or you need to make adjustments for your physical makeup. This is another principle that attracts me to Arwrology.

I believe that the sign of a master instructor is not the ability to teach someone to be like you, but teach them to be the best they can according to their individual strengths and weaknesses. Also, the biggest problem I find with training is that it is usually conducted in a sterile environment under controlled circumstances. Having someone attack you with pulled punches in a well lit and padded dojo is a lot different than someone actually trying to take your head off in a dark parking lot.

"Be Skeptical. Time and space does not permit delving into all the remote tight corners in which you might find yourself if your application of these methods happen to present new problems. So first learn the classical methods described, then tear it to pieces. In the classes of the Society of Arwrologists, we frequently have a Tear it to Pieces night, at which we try to prove that our own methods are no good."[16]

This is quite a different and refreshing approach to training than the traditional "the grandmaster's way" or "the highway ryu". Not that there is anything wrong with traditional training.On the contrary it is excellent for learning usable fighting skills. The problem is that some of those fighting skills may not be for you, so if you're solely training for self-defense and preservation of your life, why practice them?

To continue in this vein let's move to one of the reasons why we need to be skeptical-the difference in your and the opponent's physical makeup.

Individual Differences

Another principle that attracted me to Arwrology and verified my own thoughts on hand-to-hand fighting was that each person is an individual and therefore has different strengths and weaknesses. The job of an instructor is to identify those weaknesses and either help the student to improve them or eliminate them completely. On the other hand the instructor should identify the strengths and help the student to enhance them so he can become a more effective fighter.

The goal of Arwrology is to give the students tools so they will have the self-confidence to effectively fight for their freedoms. If they are training in methods that are not suited for them as an individual then how can that instill self-confidence in their fighting ability?

PRINCIPLES

"The psychological effect of possessing a working knowledge of Arwrology is bound to give soldier and civilian alike, a sense of security which in turn will help to foster in him initiative, fearlessness and self-confidence."[17]

You can't expect a 5'6" man to strike a 6'5" man effectively in the side of the neck with a backhand elbow blow. But he can strike him effectively with a backhand edge hand blow. Dr. Perrigard understood that what might work for one person, may not work for another. Therefore you need to have the freedom and ability to adjust the methods to suit your needs.

"Individual Differences. Because of the differences in size, weight and strength, among students and opponents, slight variations may be used, governed by the individual need. Employ group practice. Experiment with all methods, adding little points to suit your particular physique and ability."[18]

Be Too Careful

Arwrology is a dangerous science. Its methods can DISABLE and KILL. I counsel you to be extremely careful when practicing the methods with your partner, especially the blows and death locks. Save the full speed, full power training for the striking pads and training mannequins. A little enthusiasm with your partner can change life forever. I can assure you that it is not something you want to carry with you the rest of your life here on earth.

ALWAYS BE TOO CAREFUL!

"Too much emphasis cannot be placed on care when practicing the methods which will follow. Great strength is not prerequisite for this science. Necks and hearts may be broken easily by premature enthusiasm or horseplay."[19]

NOTES

CHAPTER 2

CONDITIONING

Psycho-Physical Calisthenics

In his book Arwrology, Dr. Perrigard mentions the practice of Psycho-Physical Calisthenics. These are individual combat conditioning exercises that not only help develop automatic conditioned reflexes, but also have the psychological effect of developing self-confidence.

It was Dr. Perrigard's belief that in order to develop automatic conditioned reflexes that are so needed in fighting, the body needs to constantly repeat those actions. He felt that a way of achieving this is by substituting all of non-fighting related calisthenics for those that are more combat oriented.

"Exercise should be designed to quicken "fighting" reflexes so the correct "fighting" reactions will become automatic. The exercise motions should have a conterminous relationship with the motion to be used in actual fighting."[1].

Does this mean that we should not do general strength and cardio-vascular type exercises like push-ups, sit-ups, pull-ups and running? No, I would think they have their place in not only developing general health through physical fitness, but the results of that training could be also used as a guide to a person's degree of strength and stamina. I believe what Dr. Perrigard was alluding to is the use of non essential combat related exercise and ceremonial drill which he felt was a waste of time compared to the need for those exercises that develop close combat skills.

AMERICAN ARWROLOGY

*"The psycho-physical calisthenics of this science can develop individual groups of muscles to an extraordinary degree of efficiency and it can give the student a specialized neuro-muscular co-ordination so necessary in unarmed combat."*2

Besides the obvious physical advantages of developing neuro-muscular co-ordination and automatic conditioned reflexes for fighting, Arwrology Psycho-Physical Calisthenics also have a psychological aspect.

*"One of the main (Arwrology) features is psychological. It gives a man a feeling of self-confidence. Like an imaginary gun at his belt, it is always ready to assist him when he tries 'to do right as he sees right.' The psychological effect of possessing a working knowledge of Arwrology is bound to give a soldier and civilian alike a sense of security which in turn will help to foster in initiative, fearlessness and self-confidence."*3

Dr. Perrigard makes a case in regards to changing the manner in which the military trained its personnel. His feeling was that instead of having them do repetitions of calisthenics that have nothing to do with movements of combat, the soldier should be repeating fighting related movements to not only condition their bodies and help develop automatic conditioned reflexes, but also give them the confidence to know that they can handle themselves in a violent situation when the need arises.

Dr. Perrigard's fellow Arwrologists included members of police, military and special intelligence units. Therefore, he was familiar with the training practices of various combat oriented organizations. As a physician he understood the effects of fatigue and stress on the mind and body, and therefore the need for exercise to develop conditioned reflex. Because of this he came up with a series of calisthenics geared for violent situations. They included: crawling, throwing yourself to the ground for cover, quickly rising from a seated cross -legged position, carrying a wounded comrade and unarmed striking exercises.

CONDITIONING

"Instead of the generalized exercises with archaic knee bending and arm raising motions, directed at no specific future action on the battlefield, in the street, or in the concentration camp, there should be a series of exercises which will serve some specific duty in actual combat, and help the solider, on battlefields."[4]

Dr. Perrigard authored Arwrology for the fighting man, whether he was a member of an elite intelligence unit operating on foreign soil, or a member of the Home Guard protecting his own country's borders. But he also addressed civilians, and their need for an automatic conditioned reflex method of combat to provide them with fighting skills and confidence to survive a violent attack. The following conditioning exercises are a combination of what I've learned from over the three decades of training and research to include Dr. Perrigard and the Society of Arwrologists.

Although each exercise has a specific purpose targeting certain neuro-muscular development, they all have a common goal – development of automatic conditioned reflexes for fighting to give the student the skills and confidence to face a deadly threat.

Body Whips

Approximately 15 years ago I was diagnosed with cancer which required open chest surgery and extensive in-patient chemo-therapy. This rendered me unable to practice my beloved hand-to-hand combat. The chemo left me very weak and I didn't have the physical ability to train at the dynamic intensity required for proper execution of technique. Through research and inquiry I started practicing Tai Chi Chuan because it consisted of soft movements which did not require a high level of energy of which I was totally void. During this period I was introduced to a series of exercises used to condition the body for Tai Chi training. I soon discovered that not only did some of these exercise parallel the body motion in my hand-to-hand training they also had health benefits. I call them Body Whips.

AMERICAN ARWROLOGY

Body whips are three motion exercises derived from the Chinese martial arts that parallel movement in hand-to-hand fighting. The three exercises are called Front Whip, Side & Leg Whip. I will get into the actual exercises and their application below but first I want to explain why I think these exercises are an absolute must for any training regimen.

These exercises are not Arwrology per se, but a part of my American Arwrology daily training routine. They are my interpretation of what I researched to help keep my body toned and conditioned for fighting while unable to train in hand-to-hand combat. But, it is interesting to note Dr. Perrigard's successor Second Regent Michael Thomson does practice Chinese internal arts to supplement his daily training regimen. The reason I've added Body Whips to my daily training routine is because: they aid in your development of the muscles, tendons and ligaments used in hand-to-hand combat; they parallel the movement of hand-to-hand combat thus aiding in your development of automatic conditioned reflexes; and they benefit your health by increasing your energy and aiding in the proper function of your organs.

Hand-to-hand fighting consists of many forms of movement. For training purposes I would like to put them into three main categories: moving forward and back, moving to the side, and turning forward and back. These will be explained later in the details of the individual exercises. Body Whips help tone and develop particular muscles that create those hand-to-hand movements. They massage, stretch and tone the joint muscles, tendons and ligaments to prepare your body for the more explosive methods of Arwrology. And they do it with very little energy and zero stress on the body. In fact, it is actually relaxing to perform these exercises.

The main goal of Arwrology is for you to develop automatic conditioned reflexes for hand-to-hand fighting. What better way to start your day than to begin by doing a series of soft, relaxing exercises that take little time and energy, while increasing your fighting skills and making your body healthier. It's a win-win situation.

By paralleling your hand-to-hand movements, the Body Whips will aid in conditioning your reflexes to respond automatically when the need

16

CONDITIONING

arises. A benefit of doing these exercises the first thing in the morning is they are soft and don't require a great amount of energy. Let's face it; some of us are just not morning training people. Also, they are not time consuming, taking approximately only five minutes to complete from start to finish. And, if you're a very busy person you may not get to your hand-to-hand training session so at least you've done something to help develop your reflexes.

When I was practicing Tai Chi Chuan I discovered that these exercises have many health advantages besides muscle toning and development. Some of this lies in the mysteries of internal energy flow of which I am not an expert. It is believed that the movements of the exercises open the meridian gates which allow natural energy to flow freely throughout the body. It is also believed that regular daily linear movement does not allow the organs to be properly massaged thus restricting them from operating at 100% efficiency. The circular twisting movements of the Body Whip will aid in massaging the organs and increase the function of the various organs especially those of the digestive system. Coupled with proper breathing methods you will also reap respiratory benefits as well.

The following is a detailed description of the three Body Whips that I have chosen to supplement American Arwrology. I suggest doing these every morning almost immediately after you rise from bed. Doing twenty-four repetitions of each exercise will take approximately five to six minutes. If you have more time you may increase the repetitions. But don't let it become a burden to the point of giving up. Enjoy the time. Do less, rather than none. The idea is to do them every single day. Do the movements slowly and soft. They should be round and fluid moving like water. Inhale and exhale through the nose. Breathe deeply and time your breaths with the body movements. This will oxidize your system and clear your sinus tract. You will feel more energized in the morning. Your muscles and tendons will be stretched and toned. You will develop your automatic fighting reflexes. Your overall health will increase. And best of all – if your busy schedule does not allow you to train later in the day, at least you did something.

AMERICAN ARWROLOGY

The Front Whip

The Front Whip is an exercise that conditions the muscles that make the body move forward and back. In this exercise the body is positioned in a forward stance and rocks back and forth via pulling with the leg muscles (muscles don't push). The forward rock can be used for advancing the body forward for an attack or for a pushing type movement. The backward rock can be used for avoiding an attack or a pulling type of movement.

Besides the body moving back and forth there is movement of the arms that correspond with the motion of the body. As the body rocks forward the arms will move forward as if pushing air forward. As the body rocks back the arms will be drawn in as if scooping air and pulling it into the body.

Before I go into the mechanics of the Front Whip it is important to emphasize that this is a soft exercise and therefore all movements will be void of linear, straight, hard motion.

Imagine a large, slow, spinning wheel directly in front of your torso with a diameter ranging from your chin to your groin. The wheel is spinning away from your body - the top of the wheel moving forward away from your body and the bottom of the wheel moving back towards your body. Now imagine a stick poking through the wheel near the radius with both of your hands grabbing it one on each side of the wheel. Now with that stick use your hands to move the wheel. Starting from hands down position you will pull the wheel up towards your chin then rotate your palms forward and push the wheel forward. When your hands reach maximum forward motion they will move down and you will start the pulling motion to spin the wheel back towards your body. As your hands reach your body you will begin to pull up to repeat the wheels circular, forward motion.

The Front Whip starts with a natural stance, hands down at your side (Fig.1). Stay relaxed. You want to think soft and relaxed. Begin by inhaling through your nose and simultaneously begin to pull the wheel handles upward towards your chin. As they reach your chin start to exhale through your nose

CONDITIONING

while simultaneously taking a natural soft, step forward with your left foot as your palms rotate away from you and you push the wheel forward (Fig.2).

As your hands push forward your whole body should rock forward. As your hands reach their maximum forward position begin to inhale through your nose and simultaneously rock back as your hands are pulling the bottom of the wheel back towards your body, (Fig.3).

Fig 1.

Fig 2.

Fig 3.

Then begin to exhale as you rock forward and simultaneously push the top of the wheel forward. Repeat this motion for twelve rotations of the wheel.

The rocking motion of the Front Whip is not a leaning back and forth. The upper torso will stay vertical at all times. The spine should be vertical and completely straight for all Body Whip exercises. The forward and back rocking is caused by the movement of your legs. To rock forward you push forward with the rear leg until your torso is over your bent knee. Approximately eighty percent of your weight will be supported by the front leg. To rock back you push backward with the front leg until your torso is over your rear bent knee. Again, approximately eighty percent of your weight will be supported by the rear leg.

On the pulling back motion of the twelfth rotation bring your left foot back to a natural stance and then step forward with your right foot to start the next twelve rotations. What you are doing is twelve rotations on each side.

The Front Whip is an excellent exercise for health and developing automatic conditioned reflexes. The movement duplicates those for pre-emptive unarmed strikes such as the tiger claw and edge hand blows. It can also be used for clearing a garment and drawing a weapon from a concealed appendix carry position. It should take approximately two minutes to complete both sides. This averages out to about five seconds per rotation. If you go under three seconds per rotation you are moving too fast for this type exercise. Don't rush it or you'll miss out on all the benefits.

The Side Whip

The Side Whip is an exercise which conditions the muscles that make the body twist and move from side to side. In this exercise the body is positioned in a natural stance with feet pointed forward. The body rocks side to side via pulling with leg muscles. The difference between the previous exercise and the Side Whip is that the upper torso twists as it is rocking side to side.

CONDITIONING

This moving to the side and twisting motion can be used to generate power for offensive forehand and backhand striking type blows. The same motion can be used for throws, chokes and counter weapon techniques. It can also be used defensively for avoiding straight on attacks such as a knife thrust.

As with the previous exercise, the Side Whip also incorporates movement of the arms. Arm motion will be a soft whipping action which will occur naturally from the twisting motion of the torso. As the torso twists forward the foremost arm will naturally swing in that direction.

As with the Body Whips, the Side Whip is a soft flowing exercise. It should feel like water whipping through a winding creek. Keep the body as relaxed as possible. As the body is twisting forward and back let the whipping arm naturally swing out about forty-five degrees away from the body. Keep the spine vertical throughout the exercise.

The Side Whip exercise is done in two stages: the forehand whip and the backhand whip. I will start with the Forehand Side Whip.

The Side Whip begins from a natural stance. The feet should be spaced apart slightly wider than shoulder width. Point the feet forward. Keep the spine straight. Relax the arms as they hang down at your side, (Fig.4).

Fig 4.

As with all the Body Whips, while performing you will breathe through your nose. Inhale on one movement, exhale on the next. For the forehand side whip you will begin by inhaling and rocking over to your left placing approximately eighty percent of your weight over your left leg. Do not move your feet. Twist your torso until you are facing right (Fig.5). Begin to rock forward over to the right as you exhale through your nose. When your weight is over your right leg begin to whip your torso forward around to the left until you are facing left. Let your right arm whip naturally in a forehand motion around to the left at approximately forty - five degrees away from the body, (Fig.6). Repeat this series twelve times without stopping the motion.

Fig 5.

Fig 6.

The Backhand Side Whip is just the opposite of the Forehand Side Whip. Instead of rocking forward and whipping the forehand you will be rocking backward and whipping the backhand.

CONDITIONING

Begin by inhaling and rocking over to your left placing approximately eighty percent of your weight on your left leg. Do not move your feet. Twist your torso until you are facing left, (Fig.7). Begin to rock backward over to the right as you exhale through your nose. When your weight is over your right leg begin to whip your torso backward around to the right until you are facing right, (Fig.8). Let your right arm whip naturally in a backhand motion around to the right at approximately forty - five degrees away from the body. Don't raise it higher. Let it whip out and around naturally. Begin rocking backward to the left as you inhale through the nose.

Fig 7.

Fig 8.

When your weight is over your left leg begin to whip your torso backward around to the left until you are facing the left, (Fig.9).

Let your left arm whip naturally in a backhand motion around to the left approximately forty-five degrees away from the body. Repeat this series twelve times without stopping the motion.

The total Side Whip exercise should take you approximately two minutes to complete. Ideal timing is two seconds for an inhale and two seconds for an exhale. Keep the motion soft, round and fluid. Side to side movement should be very slow and add slight speed and momentum to the whips.

Fig 9.

This is an excellent exercise for massaging the organs and increasing energy flow. Keep it smooth and slow and reap the benefits.

The Leg Whip

The Leg Whip is an exercise which conditions the muscles that makes the legs move to the front and rear. This is extremely simple exercise that aids in the development of balance and automatic conditioned reflexes for the knee, toe and heel strikes. It also has the health benefits of aiding in the function of the digestive tract.

From a natural stance, lift one foot slightly off the ground balancing all your weight on the opposite leg. If you have trouble with keeping your balance you may hold on to a chair or wall. As you progress in your training hold the chair or wall with a lighter touch until you no longer need the assistance, (Fig.10).

CONDITIONING

Fig 10.

Fig 11.

Pull back the lifted leg as far as you are comfortably able without bending the torso. Remember to keep the torso upright and spine straight. Bend the knee until the lower leg is approximately parallel with the ground. Inhale through the nose as you pull the leg back, (Fig.11). Then as you exhale swing the leg forward until your thigh is parallel with the ground. The lower leg should be extended but comfortable. The foot should be pulled back with the toes pointed upward at the end of the forward swing, (Fig.12).

Repeat the front to rear Leg Whip twenty - four times on each side.

Fig 12.

Stay relaxed throughout this exercise. Your leg should be like a pendulum's natural weight creating the momentum. If you feel a slight muscle pull in your thighs, you are forcing the leg higher than it wants to go. Let the height of the front and rear swing progress naturally as your body gets used to the movement. Time your inhales with the rearward movement and your exhales with forward movement. Each complete front to rear swing should take approximately two seconds. Again, any faster and you're missing out on the benefits. Keep it soft, slow and fluid.

Knee Blow Drill

Arwrology is a close-in hand-to-hand fighting art. Therefore, you need to condition natural weapons that work in-close. Without a doubt the best in-close leg striking technique is the knee blow. Not only is it simple and natural to execute but it also has many target applications.

The Knee Blow Drill has three purposes all of which directly relates to hand-to-hand fighting. Purpose 1: The striking movement aids in developing the fast twitch muscles that are needed to quickly and powerfully deliver knee blows. Purpose 2: The retraction movement aids in developing forward momentum in the strikes to retain an aggressive fighting offense. Purpose 3: The repetition of the movement aids in developing automatic conditioned reflexes.

The Drill

Stand natural with your feet shoulder width apart pointing forward and your arms hanging relaxed down at your sides. Snuggly press your elbows against the sides of your torso to keep the upper arm stationary. Bend your elbows raising your lower arms up and out in front of your body with your palms facing down.

CONDITIONING

Fig 13.

This is the starting position for the knee blow drill, (Fig.13). Now, like a bullet being shot out of a barrel raise your left knee and strike your out-stretched left palm. Do not move the hand down to strike the knee. Let the knee strike the stationary palm. As fast as you struck the palm drop the foot straight down to the floor at the point below the palm, (Fig.14). Now, repeat the strike and retraction with the right knee, (Fig.15).

Fig 14.

Fig 15.

Your feet from toe to toe should be about twelve to fifteen inches apart. Keep repeating the knee blows to the palms, one after another, until you reach the pre-determined workout repetitions.

As previously mentioned one of the benefits of the Knee Blow Drill is to develop automatic conditioned reflexes. This can only be done by a set amount of repetitions repeated daily over an extended period of time. I recommend 25 per side, per day, every day. Less is too little, more is too much. Do not overdo the drill as it will become laborious and easily forgotten. Make it fast, lively and fun. The whole drill, 25 repetitions on each side should not take longer than 60 seconds.

Dr. Perrigard was very adamant about making your drills as realistic as possible by thinking that you are actually striking someone's crotch, stomach or face if they are bent over. This will increase the intensity of the knee blow drill. The constant quick repetition will also train your body to deliver multiple driving forward blows when applicable.

"Every time you strike your knee up, think of giving mighty knee blows up at your enemy's stomach or crotch. And in actual fighting, keep your knees driving into your opponent at every opportunity."[5]

Edge of Hand Wall Drill

Another effective natural weapon to Arwrology's close-in hand-to-hand fighting art is the Edge of Hand. Dr. Perrigard, along with numerous other WW2 era Close Combat instructors thought the Edge of Hand Blow was the deadliest of the unarmed striking techniques. *"The edge hand is the most deadly natural weapon that an unarmed man possess if he knows how to use it."*[6]

CONDITIONING

The formation of the Edge of Hand is fingers extended, thumb down and palm nearly always facing down. The thumb is kept close to the hand because The Doc believed extending the thumb causes vibrations like a tuning fork which could lead to severe joint damage. The striking surface will be the portion of the hand between the wrist and the knuckle of the pinky finger. When the Edge of Hand is delivered keep the wrist and forearm straight which has less give to the technique. Dr. Perrigard makes references to the Edge of Hand Blow as a light snappy strike.

The Drill

The main purpose for the Wall Drills is to develop power for in-close fighting. It also emphasizes moving around the opponent by twisting and turning. Dr. Perrigard's goal was having the ability to strike effectively while moving from medium to close range. The Doc wanted his Arwr-Men to know how to strike in-close because nobody else could fight like that.

Dr. Perrigard also gives some important fighting principles for the Wall Drills. Twisting away and then turning back into your opponent using stomach muscles for power. This principle is termed Twist Unwind Torso (TUT) which is essential to The Doc's power development. This will be further discussed in Chapter 3.

What you are attempting to do is strike powerfully from an in-close position. When the movement becomes more natural you can begin striking at different angles. Conditioning should also be light at first, increase power when the hand becomes used to the exercise. Dr. Perrigard also emphasizes when applying the striking technique exhale or growl, assisting with power development. Keep the spine vertical throughout the drill.

Front Wall Drill

Stand facing the wall, feet parallel, shoulder width apart, with your toes six inches away from the wall. Form a right Edge Hand in front of your left shoulder, (Fig. 16). Strike the wall using only torso torque at 9 o'clock, (Figs. 17&18).

Fig 16.

Fig 17.

Fig 18.

CONDITIONING

Repeat the drill by forming another right Edge Hand and hold it vertical up next to the right side of your head, (Fig. 19). Strike the wall using upper body torque at 12 o'clock. To develop the upper body forward torque, move your hips slightly away from the wall, (Fig. 20). This will load the Edge Hand, then whip the hips forward to throw the upper body forward, (Fig. 21). Then using the same angles repeat the drill using your left Edge Hand. Train Both Sides.

Fig 19.

Fig 20.

Fig 21.

Side Wall Drill

Stand next to the wall, body 90 degrees to it, with your shoulder and foot touching the wall. Put your right arm straight out, shoulder height, parallel with the floor. Form a right Edge Hand with the whole length of the arm also against the wall, (Fig. 22). Bend the arm at the elbow 90 degrees until the Edge Hand is positioned in front of your left shoulder. Hold that position, (Fig.23). Now keep your right foot against the wall and slightly lean your shoulder away until you have enough clearance to execute a right Edge Hand Blow on the wall at 9 o'clock, (Fig.24). Don't bend the elbow back or move the feet. Use violent upper body torque to execute the strike, (Fig.25). Repeat the drill by training the left side.

CONDITIONING

Fig 22.

Fig 23.

Fig 24.

Fig 25.

33

Rear Wall Drill

       Stand with your back against the wall. Your feet will be parallel, shoulder width apart, with your heels two inches away from the wall. Form a right Edge Hand and hold it vertically up next to the right side of your head, (Fig.26). Strike the wall at 6 o'clock using only torso torque. Just like the front wall drill move your hips slightly forward away from the wall to develop this torque, (Figs.27 & 28). Repeat the drill by forming another right Edge Hand and again hold it vertical to the right side of the head, (Fig.29). Now launch a horizontal Edge Hand at 9 o'clock only using upper body torque, (Figs.30 & 31). Repeat the drill by training the left side.

Fig 26.

CONDITIONING

Fig 27.

Fig 28.

Fig 29.

Fig 30.

The Wall Drills described here are basic. Once the body movements become natural begin to practice at a multitude of angles. Five to ten repetitions with full power impact each training session is good enough.

Training twice per week is plenty, anything over that is a waste of time and not necessary for Combat. You are training to win a violent encounter not a Kata competition.

Fig 31.

NOTES

37

CHAPTER 3

BLOW POWER
D-55

Natural Weapons

"Blow Power acts as a speedy prelude to your Holds."[1]

Backhand Elbow (BHEB): The striking area is the back tip of the elbow. The arm is always kept loose and always strike violently through the target. (Fig.32 & 33)

Fig 32.

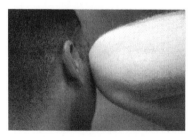

Fig 33.

Backhand Edge Hand (BHEH): The weapon is the pinkie side of the hand between the wrist and the knuckle. Extend the fingers, thumb down, and tighten hand upon impact.(Fig.34 & 35)

Fig 35.

Fig 35.

Vertical Fist (VF): The weapon is the first knuckle of the index and middle fingers. The hand is formed by making a convulsive fist; the thumb is bent and held against the second and third knuckle of the index and middle finger. Your forearm and wrist alignment is flat on top and to the outside. The fist will be chambered next to the torso.(Fig.36 & 37)

Tiger Claw (TC): The weapon includes all of your finger tips. The hand is formed as if you were holding a softball or a grapefruit. The hand and arm is held loose, tighten fingers upon impact.(Fig.38 & 39)

Fig 36.

Fig 37.

Fig 38.

Fig 39.

Palm Heel (PH): The weapon is the portion of the palm nearest the wrist. The hand formation is just like the tiger claw with the wrist full back exposing the palm. The weapon is chambered close to the body with the elbow bent. The weapon will travel straight and vertical through the target. (Fig.40 & 41).

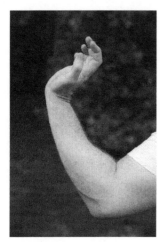

Fig 40.

Fig 41.

Forehand Elbow (FHEB): The weapon striking area is the front tip of the elbow. The weapon can be effectively launched in all directions. (Fig.42 & 43).

42

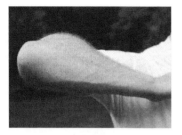

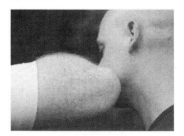

Fig 42.   **Fig 43.**

Knee (KN): The weapon is the tip of the bent knee. The weapon is launched by an explosive pulling up of the thigh and pushing forward with the hips. (Fig.44 & 45).

Fig 44.   **Fig 45.**

Toe Kick (TK): The weapon is the toes of the foot. The foot is launched by an explosive pulling up of the thigh and a whipping forward motion of the lower leg. The ankle is kept bent upward throughout the strike. (Fig.46 & 47).

Fig 46.

Fig 47.

Heel Kick (HK): The weapon is the heel of the foot. Weapon is chambered by lifting the bent knee up to the chest. The weapon is launched by a stomping motion downward. The ankle is bent throughout the strike.(Fig.48 & 49).

Fig 48.

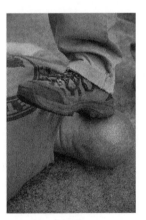

Fig 49.

BLOW POWER: D-55

Stomp Kick (SK): The weapon is the outside portion of the foot directly under the leg. The weapon is chambered by lifting the knee to the opposite shoulder and is launched by a stomping motion downward. (Fig.50 & 51).

Fig 50.   **Fig 51.**

Targets
Under the stresses of combat or a violent street attack don't be specific with targets on the body. *"Hit your opponent with everything you got."*2

Target Bands
I have dissected the body into three circular bands. There are effective targets within each of these bands, 360 degrees around the human body. Target Band 1 includes the head to the shoulders. Target Band 2 is the shoulders to lower abdomen and Target Band 3 will include the lower abdominal area to the feet.

AMERICAN ARWROLOGY

Target Band 1: The Head (Fig.33), Carotid Sinus (Fig.35), Temple, Eyes (Fig.39), Jaw (Fig.41), Throat (Fig.43), and the Back of the Neck (Fig.49).

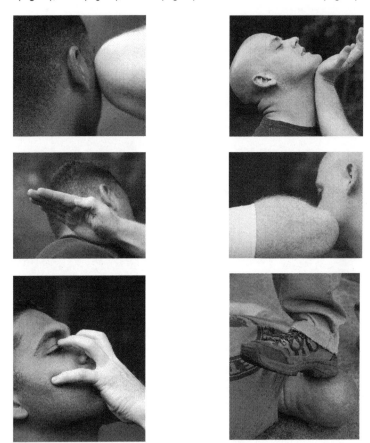

Left column (top to bottom): Figs 33, 35, & 39.
Right column (top to bottom): Figs 41, 43 & 49.

46

Target Band 2: The Solar Plexus, Spine, Lower Abdominal, Floating Ribs and the Small of the Back. (Fig.37) (Fig.45)

Fig 37.

Fig 45.

Target Band 3: Groin and Knee (Fig.37) (Fig.45) (above), (Fig.47), (Fig.51) (below).

Fig 47.

Fig 51.

Principles of Power Development

SWAMP: SWAMP is an acronym developed by co - founder and Master Instructor John Watson of the Gung Ho Chuan Association. For over two decades this principle of power development has been and still is an instrumental part of the GHCA's close combat curriculum.

Stay Relaxed. Being relaxed is completely necessary for your body to move quicker and more efficiently. Explosive movement doesn't come from stiff, tense muscles. Staying loose you'll find your movements to be much more dynamic.

Weapon First. Your hand or leg technique must be thrown first so not to telegraph the technique. Most importantly it allows the body to follow the weapon in, creating mass behind the strike.

Acceleration. Speed x Mass = Power. Once you move, move the weapon as fast as it is physically able to. Then don't stop until it is over! Acceleration is speed and that is developed by staying relaxed.

Move in the direction of the blow. Your body needs to move in the same direction as your blow. This can only be accomplished by throwing the weapon first and moving the body in the same direction of the strike.

Plunge. This is throwing all your body weight into the technique. The weapon must hit before your body mass.

Each one of these principles supports the other. Lose one of them and you'll have a dramatic loss in explosive blow power.3

Twist Unwind Torso

In extremely close quarters you are limited in utilizing some of the more common methods of power development. To overcome this deficit, The Doc stressed the need to continuously twist and turn the body in order to generate a violent torquing motion. *"In fierce hand-to-hand fighting remember to twist and turn...twist away from your opponent and turn quickly towards him, delivering blow power."*4 The Doc also emphasized the importance of utilizing the abdominal muscles, often referred to as your "core". *"Use abdominal muscles to put power into your short blows."*5 The core which links the top and bottom halves of the body allows the upper and lower extremities to function as a single unit. A properly conditioned core will enhance limb strength and generate greater blow power. A good example of this principle, "twist unwind torso," in action is the tension created and released in your abdominals as you load and deliver strikes in the Wall Drills from Chapter 2.

D-55

Since I was first introduced to Dr. Perrigard in 1994, I've been researching his system of hand-to-hand fighting based on Samurai Jiu-Jitsu and his knowledge of the human anatomy. During my research I was sent some training videos of a WW2 Close Combat Instructor demonstrating his interpretation of hand-to-hand. I personally know this instructor and I can tell you that he is the real deal. He has about forty years under his belt and is an encyclopedia on fighting techniques. This instructor laid out a plethora of techniques in two tapes I received which raised the question – "How come so much?" What if there wasn't more – but less? Not less as we know it, but really less. This led me to some very in depth research to find the "Holy Grail" of close combat – in close fast power, minimum techniques trained to an automatic

49

conditioned reflex.

Along with the physical research was the academic research, that included forty Jiu-Jitsu and close combat book reviews spanning from 1904-1973. Also, there are pages and pages of notes from telecoms with our Canadian Forefather – Mike Thomson. When I got to the end of my book research the light bulb came on and my research took a totally different turn from where I planned to go – I truly believe I found the Holy-Close-Combat-Grail. Finally and after 36 years of training, it's not targets, it's not weapons, it's not the attack, it's not power development, it's not attitude. Yes, all those are important but only a part of the big picture -

AUTOMATIC CONDITIONED REFLEXES.

Automatic Conditioned Reflex training is training with simplistic attack sequences on both sides of the body to the point of responding automatically to any violent action, hence-D-55.

So where did D-55 originate from? The letter D is for drill and 55 comes from the bag drill demonstrated in Dr. Perrigard's book Arwrology on page 55. The purpose of D-55 is to practice and develop automatic conditioned reflex to speed up your fighting movements. The great thing about the D-55 drill is that you will be training both sides of the body whether you want to or not. In the later Chapters when the Throws, Chokes and the Dragon Knife Fighting are discussed Automatic Conditioned Reflexes is not the weapon motion that is exactly applied but the same body motion. D-55 will provide you with the same body motion conditioning for a violent confrontation.

D-55 Drill

Start the drill by marking an area off no larger than six feet. During the drill keep your techniques within this six foot area.

BLOW POWER: D-55

The techniques should be started off slowly then in time increase your speed and intensity. If you find you need to catch up to your body during the drill it's not realistic for in-close fighting, slow down.

Training Notes:

After striking with the Backhand Edge Hand it leaves your back hip forward. In order to generate power to the next strike, the Vertical Fist, you have to re-chamber the hip. Care must be taken to make sure you are not missing the hip chambering. If so the Vertical Fist will be just arm strength.

The Vertical Fist and Knee are not thrown at the exact time. The fist chambers the knee for a 1-2 combination.

At an advanced stage in Conditioned Reflex training your body power movements should become small, they should be very quick, tight turns to create body torque. Techniques should be very close *"Love thy enemy with no room for large arm motion."*

When fighting don't fight your enemy's fight, *"Be Unorthodox."*

On the following two pages:

> Left Backhand Elbow (Fig.52)
> Left Backhand Edge Hand (Fig.53)
> Right Vertical Fist (Fig.54)
> Right Knee (Fig.55)
> Right Forehand Elbow (Fig.56)
>
> Right Backhand Elbow (Fig.57)
> Right Backhand Edge Hand (Fig.58)
> Left Vertical Fist(Fig.59)
> Left Knee (Fig.60)
> Left Forehand Elbow (Fig.61)

Fig 52.

Fig 53.

Fig 54.

Fig 55.

Fig 56.

BLOW POWER: D-55

Fig 57.

Fig 58.

Fig 59.

Fig 60.

Fig 61.

Impact

After mastering the motion study of D-55 it is important to include impact training. For the best results, work with a hanging heavy bag. The movement of the bag may mimic what your enemy's body will do during in-close fighting. These movements will force you to apply the Principles of Power Development.

"Repeat the cycle of blows over and over until you have attained your maximum speed. Deliver hard blows; keep pressing forward at all times."[6]

NOTES

CHAPTER 4

ATTACK DRILLS

Introduction

The Attack Drills in this Chapter are simply the next turn in the "Endless Knot" of American Arwrology. In the previous Chapter you learned the essential movements (D-55) that are the core of Automatic Conditioned Reflexes necessary for success in a violent encounter. Through slight variations of the D-55 drill one is able to incorporate the remainder of the natural weapons and make them part of your Automatic Conditioned Arsenal.

Remember the goal is to have at your disposal an endless number of deadly strikes, throws and holds, so if one method happens to fail another is ready to take its place immediately.

The Attack Drills

Any number after D-55 is either a hand for hand replacement of a foot for a foot replacement.

Any number before D-55 would mean that the technique starts the drill with a pre-emptive strike.

D-55-5

Left Backhand Elbow (Fig.62), Left Backhand Edge Hand (Fig.63), Right Palm Heel (Fig.64), Right Knee(Fig.65), Right Forehand Elbow (Fig.66).

Fig 62.

Fig 63.

Fig 64.

Fig 65.

Fig 66.

ATTACK DRILLS

D-55-5

Right Backhand Elbow (Fig.67), Right Backhand Edge Hand(Fig.68), Left Palm Heel (Fig.69), Left Knee (Fig.70), Left Forehand Elbow (Fig.71).

Fig 67.

Fig 68.

Fig 69.

Fig 70.

Fig 71.

D-55-8

Left Backhand Elbow (Fig.72), Left Backhand Edge Hand (Fig.73), Right Vertical Fist (Fig.74), Right Toe Kick (Fig.75), Right Forehand Elbow (Fig.76).

Fig 72.

Fig 73.

Fig 74.

Fig 75.

Fig 76.

ATTACK DRILLS

D-55-8

Right Backhand Elbow (Fig.77), Right Backhand Edge Hand (Fig.78), Left Vertical Fist (Fig79), Left Toe Kick (Fig.80), Left Forehand Elbow (Fig.81).

Fig 77.   Fig 78.

Fig 79.   Fig 80.   Fig 81.

2-D-55

Left Pre-Emptive Edge Hand (Fig.82), Right Vertical Fist (Fig.83), Right Knee (Fig.84), Right Forehand Elbow (Fig.85), Right Backhand Edge Hand (Fig.86).

Fig 82.

Fig 83.

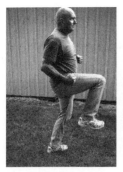

Fig 84.

Fig 85.

Fig 86.

ATTACK DRILLS

2-D-55

Right Pre-Emptive Edge Hand (Fig.87), Left Vertical Fist (Fig.88), Left Knee (Fig.89), Left Forehand Elbow (Fig.90), Left Backhand Edge Hand (Fig.91).

Fig 87.

Fig 88.

Fig 89.

Fig 90.

Fig 91.

4-D-55

Left Pre-Emptive Tiger Claw (Fig.92), Right Vertical Fist (Fig.93), Right Knee (Fig.94), Right Forehand Elbow (Fig95), Right Backhand Edge Hand (Fig.96).

Fig 92.

Fig 93.

Fig 94.

Fig 95.

Fig 96.

ATTACK DRILLS

4-D-55
Right Pre-Emptive Tiger Claw (Fig.97), Left Vertical Fist (Fig.98), Left Knee (Fig.99), Left Forehand Elbow (Fig.100), Left Backhand Edge Hand (Fig.101).

Fig 97.

Fig 98.

Fig 99.

Fig 100.

Fig 101.

10-D-55

Left Stomp Kick (Fig.102), Left Backhand Elbow (Fig.103), Left Backhand Edge Hand (Fig.104), Right Vertical Fist (Fig.105), Right Knee (Fig.106), Right Forehand Elbow (Fig.107).

Fig 102.

Fig 103.

Fig 104.

Fig 105.

Fig 106.

Fig 107.

ATTACK DRILLS

10-D-55

Right Stomp Kick (Fig.108), Right Backhand Elbow (Fig.109), Right Backhand Edge Hand (Fig.110), Left Vertical Fist (Fig.111), Left Knee (Fig.112), Left Fore-hand Elbow (Fig.113).

Fig 108.

Fig 109.

Fig 110.

Fig 111.

Fig 112.

Fig 113.

AMERICAN ARWROLOGY

Pre-Emptive Training

Why? You deliver an explosive strike before your adversary does. Therefore your adversary will be hit before he can counter the attack. The theory is a simple one; action is faster than reaction.

Here is an exercise to develop non-telegraphing pre-emptive strikes. Stand in front of a full length mirror and get into a combat stance. The stance should allow you to explode into action using either arm or leg. Choose one of the natural weapons to work on. Now watch yourself in the mirror and deliver the technique while concentrating on not telegraphing the strike. When starting this exercise execute the technique slowly until it becomes natural. Repeat the drill over and over then gradually increase speed.

Watch the mirror to pick up on any telegraphing. Look for facial expressions; see if any part of your body is moving before the weapon or anything that will give away that you're about to strike. Once you're comfortable with the exercise move onto a training partner. Have them watch to see if you are telegraphing. Take turns doing this exercise and evaluate how to remove wasted motion and focus on quick powerful strikes.

ATTACK DRILLS

Does it Work?

Yes! GB2, ASA member was traveling along a busy interstate on the East Coast. The ASA member made a rest stop and headed to the food pavilion. While moving through a crowd GB2 brushed shoulders with a passer-by. GB2 immediately excused himself and apologized. Passer-by replied "watch where you're going!" GB2 once again apologized and the passer-by quickly replied "Asshole" and aggressively approached the Arwr-man. Passer-by was met with a pre-emptive edge hand to the side of the neck, with an ice cream cone face smash to follow; passer-by simply fell to the floor.

NOTES

CHAPTER 5

THROWS

Introduction

When training, begin slowly at first until the throwing techniques become natural. Even then because of the violent vertical dropping of the body, the head and lower back is prone to severe injury.
Be Too Careful!

Training Notes

- Always remember Blow Power
- When your enemy is down, Stomp!
- If the technique fails, strike
- If the enemy counters with a Head Lock grab the groin
- If the throw breaks down, stop and execute Blow Power to regain control.

Neck Lock Takedown

Scenario: You find yourself on your adversary's flank or you've avoided a weapon attack and now need to counter. This technique works from both sides. Train Both Sides.

The first part of the Neck Lock Takedown is a ridge hand strike to the back of the neck. Ideally this area is where the base of the skull and the neck meets.

71

AMERICAN ARWROLOGY

Reach around the back of the enemy's neck and grab his chin, face or throat, (Fig.114).

Fig 114.

The key for an effective Neck Lock is the placement and movement of the elbow. Your elbow must be vertical to your enemy's spine. Violently drop the elbow down the spine; this will lock the neck, (Fig.115). There is the possibility of your enemy escaping, to avoid this grab your enemy's upper arm with your other hand. This is also very important in holding the enemy close to you while executing the takedown.

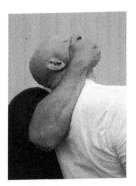

Fig 115.

THROWS

Take your leg which is on the same side as the hand that is applying the Neck Lock and launch a knee. The knee is targeting the back of your enemy's knee joint, which will start the takedown, (Fig.116). Do not lead him down! Your enemy's head should be directly in front of you and between your feet. If not, the technique is not being properly executed, (Fig.117). Follow up with Blow Power.

Fig 116.

Fig 117.

Automatic Conditioned Reflexes

As described in the earlier Chapters the purpose of D-55 is to practice and develop reflexes to speed up your fighting movement. D-55 will also provide you with the same body motion conditioning for a violent encounter. Auto-Conditioned Reflexes are not the weapon motion exactly applied but the same body motion.

When applying the Ridge Hand of the Neck Lock Take Down that movement mirrors the body motion of the Forehand Elbow of D-55. The Knee that is launched to start the takedown is the knee spike and the body movement and torqueing of the body for the takedown mirrors the Backhand Elbow.

Does it Work?

GB6, ASA member worked for a time at a busy Jersey Shore nightclub. When escorting drunk or unwanted guests to the door GB6 would walk behind them with his left hand on their left tricep, if any resistance was felt the right arm was in position for the Ridge Hand to start the Neck Lock Takedown. It was also applied on the more aggressive guy "winning" in fights. Once the Neck Lock was applied it would immediately end the problem(s).

GB79, member of the GHCA and a Law Enforcement Officer was dispatched to a violent domestic assault. As he arrived on location a juvenile ran up to him screaming his Dad was going to kill his Mom. Entering the residence GB79 found a man holding an edged weapon (straight screwdriver) to the throat of a woman. The suspect was given orders to stand down, then turned and ran up several stairs, letting go of the woman. A door opened a 10 year old girl came out crying for her Mother. GB79 tried to get the little girl to get back into her room, when the suspect turned back toward GB79 yelling "I'm going to kill you!!" The suspect lunged at GB79 with a stabbing overhand attack. The GHCA member blocked and wrapped the suspect's attacking arm while striking him with a chin jab. After a brief struggle a ridge hand was

74

thrown that immediately went into a Neck Lock Take Down. The suspect was then handcuffed.

Step Back Throw

The Step Back Throw is used to throw your enemy backwards on his head. It is purely an in-close grappling range technique and only practical after softening up your enemy with Blow Power. During the execution of the leg sweep if the adversary starts to resist use a Palm Heel to the side of the jaw.

For Demonstration purposes the Step Back Throw starts off with a Chin Jab, but is equally effective with any technique that starts pushing the adversary's body upward and back, (Fig.118).

Once you have your adversary upward and back grasp his upper arm near the elbow with your outside arm, pulling down. Simultaneously step deep (forward) to the outside of your adversary with your outside leg, (Fig.119). Target his heel with your heel, you want to throw him not trip him, (Fig. 120). Follow up with Blow Power.

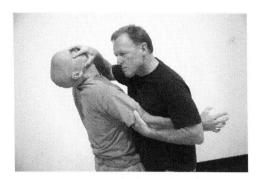

Fig 118.

Fig 119.

Fig 120.

Automatic Conditioned Reflexes
D-55-SBT

The Chin Jab is the same body motion and mirrors the Palm Heel from D-55. The violent reaping movement for the throw mirrors the Knee Strike.

THROWS

Assault Trip Throw

The Assault Trip Throw is another technique used to effectively throw your enemy backwards on his head. There are many variations of this throw but the one shown is the simplest. Improvise and Train Both Sides.

Execute a Left Knee to your enemy's leg. Target the upper thigh area (peroneal nerve). After striking with the Knee, drop that leg behind both of your enemy's legs, (Fig.121).

Fig 121.

Simultaneously extend your left arm out across the front of your enemy's body, (Fig.122). Then violently turn your body into him pushing him over your leg. Looking over your shoulder in the direction of the throw along with the violent body torque will enable a more effective throw, (Fig.123).

If the enemy counters immediately strike the groin, grab his ankles and throw him over your leg. If you find your arm behind your adversary instead of in front and across the body, execute a Forehand Elbow to the small of the back. Then finish the throw.

Fig 122.

THROWS

Fig 123.

Automatic Conditioned Reflexes
D-55-ATT

When executing the Knee to the upper thigh area it's the same body motion as the Knee Strike from D-55. The extended arm and the violent torque of the body mirrors the body motion of the Backhand Edge Hand.

AMERICAN ARWROLOGY

NOTES

CHAPTER 6

DEATH LOCKS

Introduction

In Arwrology, the most important holds are the death dealing "Arwr" locks. The Doc continually stressed the main goal to eliminate your enemy in combat were these holds. Each one is able to cause instant unconsciousness as they can quickly deplete your enemy of air or blood. If done quickly enough and with power they can dislocate and even break the neck.

BE TOO CAREFUL!

Be extremely careful when practicing these methods with your training partner. Again Arwrology is a DANGEROUS science. Practice these techniques slowly. Always double tap for immediate release, you may not be able to call out.

Posterior "Arwr" Lock

The Posterior "Arwr" Lock is a rear approach technique used to cut off your enemy's blood and air supply. Approach from the rear with your right arm straight and place your left hand on your right upper arm, (Fig.124). To soften your enemy and prevent resistance use a knee strike to the back of the leg.

Fig 124.

If using your right arm throw a right knee, (Fig.125). Violently throw both of your elbows over your enemy's shoulders.

Fig 125.

DEATH LOCKS

Immediately snake your right hand into your left elbow joint. Squeeze both elbows inward to apply pressure around your enemy's neck. Turn your left wrist down, which forms an Edge Hand to the back of his neck. Pull your elbows back cinching the noose, (Fig.126). By pulling your right elbow back you will be applying forward pressure with your left hand against the back of your enemy's neck, (Fig.127).

Fig 126.

Fig 127.

Automatic Conditioned Reflexes
D-55-PAL

When attacking from the rear, the Knee Strike to the back of the leg is the same body movement as the Knee in D-55. The arm movement over the shoulders mirrors the body movement of the Forehand Elbows. And the arm movement of closing the noose around the enemy's neck mirrors the Backhand Edge Hand.

Carotid "Arwr" Lock

The Carotid "Arwr" Lock is used to cut off the blood supply to the brain. Start by violently pushing your adversary's shoulder and simultaneously pulling the opposite elbow. It is especially effective when done with Charlie Nelson's Hi-Low Spin, (Fig.128).

Fig 128.

DEATH LOCKS

Slide your right arm across the front of your enemy's neck while pushing the right shoulder. Your enemy's throat should be in the crook of your right arm, (Fig.129).

Fig 129.

Pull his left shoulder to get your body perpendicular with your enemy's. Place your right hand on the back of your neck to lock in the choke, Fig.130).

Fig 130.

By placing the locking hand on the back of your neck it helps secure the lock and it frees up the other hand for follow up striking and weapons, (Fig.131).

Fig 131.

Automatic Conditioned Reflexes
D-55-CAL

The start of the choke begins with a Hi-Low pushing, pulling movement. This movement mirrors the same body motion as the Vertical Fist or the Palm Heel. The placing of the hand on the back of your neck to lock in the choke mirrors the same body motion of the Forehand Elbow.

Does it Work?

GB6, ASA member, working as a bouncer had to break up a fight in a club involving a guy much larger than him. GB6 placed the combatant into a Carotid Lock and concentrated on keeping pressure to the side of his neck.

DEATH LOCKS

After about twenty seconds he lost consciousness and fell to the club floor. A short time later the combatant regained consciousness, was docile, did not remember what happened and walked out of the club.

GB83, GHCA member and a Law Enforcement Officer was called to a local bar for a disorderly person. As GB83 exits his patrol car the angry drunk comes out the front door and says, "Fuck You"!! The drunk continues to walk toward GB83 and begins to clench his fists. Once the angry drunk was in reach he was hit with a Hi-Low spin and placed into a choke, which took the fight right out of him. He found some recovery in jail.

NOTES

CHAPTER 7

COUNTER HANDGUN

Introduction

When it comes to combative skill training counter weapon techniques are probably the most difficult to execute successfully. Having a person violently in your face is one thing; when they are holding a weapon it's definitely another all together. At this moment in time your Automatic Conditioned Reflexes skills will help you survive this encounter with a successful offensive attack. And as part of the Automatic Conditioned Reflexes skill should be the Counter Weapon Principle of **ReACT**.

The acronym, **ReACT** is:

Redirect, Avoid, Counter (or Control) and Takeaway (or Takedown)

Redirect is moving the weapon away from the body. This redirecting is a simultaneous movement done in conjunction with **Avoidance**. Avoidance and Redirection creates space between the body and the weapon which will set up an immediate counter-attack. Avoid what will hurt you. You must move away from or get behind the deadliest part of the weapon.

Counter (or **Controlling**) is immediately and severely hurting your attacker by going on the offensive. At the same time control the attacker's arm which is holding the weapon. Control the situation by whatever means necessary.

Takeaway is where by severely hurting your attacker you take away their intentions. Once that is done you then take away the weapon.1
Takedown can be a culmination of the counter where the attacker finishes up on the ground restrained or not.

AMERICAN ARWROLOGY

When I started my research into Arwrology and I reviewed The Doc's Principles for Counter Handgun I truly realized that the Principles I have been following and teaching for over two decades were right on for in-close fighting. The Doc tells you a make a *"light turn"* then *"quickly pull yourself out of the way of danger, stay within reach, feint being scared or helpless"*. Then he tells you to *"explode into action"*.2

Training Notes:

Even though the handgun is the only weapon discussed in this book the Principles of ReACT can apply to most Counter Weapon situations.

The Counter Attacks are demonstrated with a right handed gun attacker. In addition to Training Both Sides, train with left hand attackers.

The gun positions which are demonstrated are (front) center chest and (back) middle of back. Once the Counter Handgun technique becomes natural for you start to train different positions around the body.

Once you have countered the attack and find yourself positioned to the attackers outside (flank) follow up with a Neck Lock Takedown, then Blow Power. If you are on the attackers inside utilize your natural weapons. The Doc advocated Kneeing or Edge Hand blows after disarm; he also advocated pistol whipping, (Fig.135). (See following pages).

Instantly follow up with strikes and then work to the Death Locks. In training NEVER complete the Counter and immediately turn the weapon back over to your training partner. There are several documented cases where a successful Counter took place on the street and due to training the gun was turned right back over to the attacker. Follow up with Blow Power.

COUNTER HANDGUN

Handgun to the Front

First redirect and avoid the weapon by twisting your torso until facing right. (This body movement is identical to the Side Whips described in Chapter 2), (Fig.132). Simultaneously using your left arm push the weapon away from your body, grab the wrist. Use the left forearm as a guide and follow up with a right Palm Heel strike to the back of the gun, (Fig.133).

When you move the weapon away in this manner you are working against the weakest part of the grip. Do not count on a disarm here. Follow through by violently twisting your torso back again working on the gun hand grip. This movement will keep the gun close to the body.

Fig 132.

Fig 133.

Now grab the gun! With a pulling and pushing movement, pull the gun hand towards your body and push the gun away from the body, disarming your attacker, (Fig.134). Follow up with Blow Power, (Fig.135).

Fig 134.

Fig 135.

Always train both sides. Take into consideration you may be on the street and a loved one, a civilian or your partner is to your right and you can't redirect the gun towards the right. There is always the chance of the gun discharging during the counter. Follow the same principles and techniques as described for moving the weapon to the right. Just redirect the gun to the left.

COUNTER HANDGUN

Handgun to the Rear

When the gun is to your back, redirect and avoid the weapon by twisting your torso until facing right. Simultaneously, with your right arm redirect the weapon away from the body. This movement is identical to the Back Hand Side Whip described in Chapter2). Maintain contact with the attacker's gun arm, (Fig.136).

Next violently lunge toward your attacker. This movement will put you behind the weapon and to the attackers outside (flank), (Fig. 137).

Fig 136.

Fig 137.

95

Handgun to the Rear (continued)

With your right arm grab and take control of the upper portion of the attacker's gun arm. The upper arm or upper lever is the portion of the arm that controls movement. The right arm is thrust between the attacker's gun arm and body, forcefully grabbing the upper lever, (Fig.138). Once under control immediately follow up with a Neck Lock Takedown, then Blow Power, (Fig.139).

Fig 138.

Fig 139.

COUNTER HANDGUN

Train Both Sides! Follow the same principles and techniques as if you were moving to the right, now move left. The only difference is your body will be to the attackers inside. Utilize your natural weapons, (Fig.140), (Fig.141), and (Fig.142).

Fig 140.

Fig 141.

Fig 142.

NOTES

CHAPTER 8

DRAGON KNIFE FIGHTING

Fig 143.

Introduction

The Canadian Society of Arwrologists logo designed in 1940 consisted of a Black Dragon. Like its namesake, the Dragon Bites (tip), Claws (edge) and strikes (pommel) its adversary. It uses the same body motion as the techniques used for unarmed combat. Many close combat systems have a knife fighting system and an unarmed combat system. Arwrology has one system because it emphasizes general body movement and not individual techniques for different weapons and attack methods. Follow this principle and the Dragon becomes a part of the body, as opposed to an extension of the body.

Targets

"Fundamentally there are two things to aim at to make a stab wound quickly fatal. 1. A large artery. 2. One of the vital organs in the body."[1]

Targets for the Dragon:
- Face
- Throat
- Carotid Artery
- Brachial Artery
- Groin
- Abdominals
- Femoral Artery
- Spleen
- Liver

ATTACK DRILLS

The Slashing Drills purpose is to develop slashing attack reflexes and target acquisition
- Vertical Slash to the centerline (Fig.144)
- High Forehand slash to neck (Fig.145)
- High Backhand slash to neck (Fig. 146)
- Low Forehand slash to abdominal area (Fig.147)
- Low Backhand slash to abdominal area (Fig. 148)

DRAGON KNIFE FIGHTING

Fig 144.

Fig 145.

Fig 146.

Fig 147.

Fig 148.

Automatic Conditioned Reflexes

The Vertical Slashing body movement mirrors the same movement as the Vertical Fist from the D-55 drill. The Forehand Slashing movements are the same as the Forehand Elbow and the Backhand Slashing mirrors the Backhand Edge from D-55.

DRAGON KNIFE FIGHTING

The Thrusting Drill is to develop thrusting attack reflexes and target acquisition.

- Vertical Thrust to the neck (Fig.149)
- High Forehand Thrust to the neck(Fig.150)
- High Backhand Thrust to the neck(Fig.151)
- Low Forehand Thrust to the abdominal area(Fig.152)
- Low Backhand Thrust to the abdominal area(Fig.153)
- Vertical Thrust to the abdominal area(Fig.154)

Fig 149.

Fig 150.

Fig 151.

Fig 152.

Fig 153.

DRAGON KNIFE FIGHTING

Fig 154.

Automatic Conditioned Reflexes

The Vertical Thrust body movement mirrors the same movement as the Vertical Fist. The Forehand Thrusting is the same as the Forehand Elbow and the Backhand Thrust mirror the Backhand Edge Hand from D-55

While doing the thrusting drills I discovered that instead of crow baring (dropping of the elbow for extraction) I would drop my weight and violently torque while keeping my arm connected to my body. This used full body weight in making a devastating wound channel instead of relying just on arm power. This movement will also set up the next strike nicely.

Counter Grab

Doc's counter to wrist grabs is exceptional and in my opinion revolutionary for its time in that The Doc was very aware of the possibility of having your wrist grabbed which is normal for someone to try and do when someone is trying to stab them.

The Counter

Begin by thrusting your training knife into the abdominal area of your partner. Your partner will grab your wrist as the knife is coming in. Your enemy may also have grabbed your wrist after you have thrust the knife into him.

Immediately start the thrusting movement again to begin a forward motion, (Fig.155). Then quickly retract the knife as you are utilizing an Edge Hand to the forearms of your enemy. This may assist loosing the grip around your wrists, (Fig.156). This movement also pins the arms to the enemy's body. Follow up with a thrust to the neck, (Fig. 157).

Fig 155.

Fig 156.

DRAGON KNIFE FIGHTING

Fig 157.

NOTES

DAILY CONDITIONING DRILLS

CONDITIONING DRILLS:

     12 Body Flow Exercises
     25 Knee Blow Calisthenics
     Wall Drills (Two Times a Week)

D-55 DRILLS

     D-55
     D-55-5
     D-55-8
     2-D-55
     4-D-55
     10-D-55

DRAGON DRILLS

     Slashing Drill
     Thrusting Drill

ENDNOTES

PREFACE

1.   Gordon E. Perrigard, M.D., Arwrology, 1943, Montreal, Renouf Publishing
        Co., Back Dust Cover

INTRODUCTION

1.   Ibid, Preface II
2.   Ibid, Introduction XIV

EPITOME

1.   Ibid, Introduction XIV

CHAPTER 1

1.   Ibid, Epitome IV
2.   Ibid, Introduction XIV
3.   Ibid, pg. 63
4.   Ibid, pg.86
5.   Ibid, pg.59
6.   Ibid, Part 1
7.   Ibid, pg. 108
8.   Ibid, pg. 36
9.   Ibid, pg. 36
10.   Ibid, pg. 67
11.   Ibid, pg. Front Dust Cover
12.   Ibid, Introduction XII
13.   Ibid, Introduction XIII
14.   Ibid, pg. 123
15.   Ibid, Introduction XIV
16.   Ibid, pg. 108
17.   Ibid, Introduction XII
18.   Ibid, Introduction XV
19.   Ibid, Introduction XIV

CHAPTER 2
1.   Ibid, pg. 63
2.   Ibid, Introduction VI
3.   Ibid, Introduction V
4.   Ibid, pg. 16
5.   Ibid, pg. 41
6.   Ibid, pg. 46
CHAPTER 3
1.   Ibid, pg. 63
2.   Ibid, pg. 43
3.   Robert Kasper, Snapping In, Vol. 4 #4, 1996 Brick N.J., GHCA, pg. 3
4.   Gordon E. Perrigard, M.D., Arwrology, 1943, Montreal, Renouf Publishing Co., pg. 58
5.   Ibid, pg. 58
6.   Ibid, pg. 55
CHAPTER 7
1.   All-Out Hand-To-Hand Fighting IG 10-05, 2001, Chinchilla, GHCA, pg. 14
2.   Gordon E. Perrigard, M.D., Arwrology, 1943, Montreal, Renouf Publishing Co., pg. 135
CHAPTER 8
1.   Ibid, pg. 159

WORKS CITED

Kasper, Robert C., Snapping In, Vol. 4 #4, Brick, GHCA, 1996

Perrigard, Gordon E., M.D., Arwrology, Montreal, Renouf Co., 1943

All-Out Hand-To-Hand Fighting IG 10-05, Chinchilla, GHCA, 2001

AMERICAN ARWROLOGY

Official Arwrology Website: www.arwrology.org

Printed in Great Britain
by Amazon

36369052R00077